10 Keys to
Financial Success:
What Every Starving Artist Should Know

by Tulasi Zimmer

10 Keys to Financial Success: What Every Starving Artist Should Know

by Tulasi Zimmer

ISBN-13: 978-0989241120
ISBN-10: 0989241122

Cover by: Tulasi Zimmer

http://tulasizimmer.com

Printed in U.S.A

CRYSTALMOON
PUBLISHING

Table of Contents

Introduction

Today, more than ever, it is possible to have a financially sustainable career as an artist (visual art, graphic design, music, writing, etc.). I and many creative people are doing it, and you can too. There's no mystery to becoming a financially successful artist. The question is, are you willing to do what it takes to become one? If you are, you simply need to elevate your passion to succeed and move beyond those who try, but give up. The term starving artist may be cliché, but it is common and you will discover in this book some of the reasons why.

Although there are many challenges to achieving a successful and financially stable art career, making a viable living as an artist is a goal that is attainable. Successful artists understand artistic talent alone is not enough to guarantee financial success. Those who are committed to the mastery of their art/craft for the long haul know ensuring the financial sustainability of their work is a worthwhile and achievable goal.

In this book, I will share with you the keys that enabled me and others to transform an art career into a financially sustainable profession. My question to you is, are you ready to step out of your comfort zone and also become a player?

I am a fine artist and many of my examples in the book will refer to the visual arts. But, you should be able to easily translate the information to fit your own creative field.

Please kindly give feedback about this book by leaving a "customer review" where you purchased it. Thank you!

Key #1
Change Your Beliefs about Making Money from Art

Both of my parents were very good artists. My mother could draw like Da Vinci and my dad was a painter and sculptor. But, neither one of them chose art as a career. In fact, my dad was opposed to me majoring in art when I was in college. I was told constantly, "You cannot make a good living as an artist." If I had adopted the same principle for myself, my life would have taken a different course. But, I chose not to allow his belief to keep me from earning a Master's degree in fine arts and having a successful career as an artist.

Are limiting financial beliefs holding you back from achieving all your financial goals as an artist? Consider how the following thoughts and beliefs affect your efforts to earn a serious income from your artwork.

- Great art and money do not mix.
- It is not possible to make a living as an artist

- It is noble to be a starving artist.
- All art should be given away for free
- Artists who make tons of money are sell-outs and not taken seriously.
- Money interrupts true creative expression.

These beliefs are financially limiting and may cause you to miss many opportunities to generate income from your art or you may not even notice them at all. If you wish to achieve greater financial stability for yourself through your art, take some time to seek out the source of your own struggle to achieving success.

Consider transforming your beliefs to something more in line with your higher good:

- Money can nurture creative expression.
- Creativity is free; supplies, equipment, musical instrument etc. are not.
- Great art is a valuable investment; and artists deserve great financial support.
- Artists who make lots of money have good business sense.
- Art is a creative endeavor, but it is also a business.

You want to begin forming beliefs that support gaining income from your art and releasing the limiting beliefs that are roadblocks to success.

Beliefs are also contagious, so it is important to choose your friends wisely. Having close associations with people who have negative beliefs about making money from art, may impede and/or sabotage your desire to succeed.

How do you know when your beliefs are producing negative consequences? Look for areas of your career where you have not been achieving your desired results even after trying many different approaches. You keep trying different actions, systems, or methods, but nothing seems to work. Most likely, a limiting belief is preventing you from achieving your goals, and no amount of action will prove effective until and unless the belief is corrected. A new belief will enable you to take different actions, thereby producing different results.

You may find it difficult to shift your beliefs at first, but like any other skill, it takes practice. You'll know when your new belief has taken root because you'll begin to act in accordance with it without even thinking about it consciously. Using the following keys in this book will also help you install new beliefs about making money from your art.

Key #2
Socialize with Artists Who Are Already Succeeding

The business of art, like any other business, is hugely social. Therefore, I highly recommend networking with other artists rather than trying to go it alone.

I find financially successful artists are generally happy to share their "secrets" of success, including how they make money from their work. Therefore, make every effort to meet and socialize with them. Join art clubs or trade associations, join online artist forums, Facebook fan pages, LinkedIn groups, attend conferences, attend galley exhibits and performances, attend workshops, and find other ways to network with successful artists in your field. It is not that difficult to do, but it does require that you make an effort.

If you always socialize with artists who are making the same or less money than you, I suggest that you set an income goal and target people who are earning close to it. For instance, in the beginning, it may be difficult to relate to the advice of someone who's earning $1M per year if you are making little or no money as an artist. You may feel more comfortable understanding and applying the advice of someone who's earning $20-40K per year. When you get comfortable at that level, try meeting with people who are earning $100K per year, and notice what they are doing differently, and keep moving up from there.

When you meet successful artists, aim to be friendly, interested, and respectfully curious, but assume equal standing as human beings. Artists are generally very comfortable discussing their work, so a great opener is to ask a specific question about their work.

Successful artists in any field typically know each other. They may not get to spend a lot of time together, but they often meet in person as a consequence of moving in similar circles. If you want to become a successful artist, networking with other pros in your field is good business. As an unknown artist in any field, it's difficult to get much exposure for your work unless you have many friends who will help get the word out. Networking is a good way for you to receive income-generating ideas and opportunities, as well as exposure, without needing one to get the other.

Key #3
Create Art People Want to Buy

Many artists are slow to adopt this important key, myself included. Early in my career I held on to the belief that if I paint it people will buy it. But very few did.

Of course, it's absolutely fine to create art that no one else will appreciate. But, if you want to get paid for your art, pay attention to what people are buying in your field. What is in demand? Then, focus on the area of overlap between what people want and how you enjoy expressing your creativity. You will likely find you can just as easily create works that align with trending demands, and still give yourself plenty of room for self-expression. You must be willing to ride the waves of public desire to be a financially successful artist.

The best way to know what is selling and trending in art is to read currents art news in your local, regional, or major newspaper, online art news, and/or subscribe to any of the major art magazines like Art Forum or Art News.

Remember your art is a product that you are selling. You cannot make money unless you have collectors wanting to buy it.

Key #4
Finish What You Start

Creating volumes of art isn't enough. To be financially successful, you must get into the habit of finishing what you start.

Many amateur artists amass sizable collections of half-finished pieces. The pros often do this too, but the pros get into the habit of finishing and showing their work.

I know when I start a painting and get interrupted before it is 70% completed it is often hard for me to pick up again with the same creative energy I began with. Instead I will often move on to a new painting. If it's 90%+ done, or if I just need to do a few touch-ups, then I'll likely finish it. Otherwise, I will store it in a closet and forget about it. I consider the value of the unfinished pieces to be learning experiences and keep my energies focused on the present, which is the only place where I can create. I prefer to keep my creative energy moving forward, than to have it stalled in the past worrying about unfinished projects.

You may feel that finishing a creative project is an unnatural process. Or a creative work is never really done — it's abandoned. It's true you can keep polishing and refining a piece indefinitely, but at some point you have to declare it done and move on. It takes practice to get a feel for when a piece should be considered finished, and there's no right or wrong approach to it. It is mainly a matter of trial and error, experience, and intuition.

When I begin a new creative work, I like to express my ideas quickly and tune out distractions until the piece is finished. I find it best to work on one creative piece at a time and to finish it as quickly as possible. Other artists work on several projects simultaneously. The important thing is to have a system in place that will allow you to create a large body of quality, finished artwork quickly.

One suggestion is to join an art movement called, Daily Painting (or artist daily), to help you create and sell finished art on a daily basis. The "daily artists" commit to creating small works of art every day, on any subject, and post it online for sale. You can sell the finished art cheaply from one of the art daily online galleries, start an art blog, sell on eBay, or on your own web site. It's a good way to bring exposure to your art and place you in front of potential collectors who will be viewing your work on a daily basis.

Key #5
Promote Your Art for Free

If you want to become a financially successful artist, you'll need to share your art with the world. Hiding the art you create in your studio or storing it in a closet, it will not generate income.

If you are just getting started in your field, I recommend that you focus on finding ways to make it visible, and don't worry too much about generating income. If you can gain visibility and sustain it, it is much easier to generate a steady income later.

One good strategy for creating visibility is to give your work away or find a business that will display your art for free. That's right! Spread it around as widely as possible. Encourage people to share it with no restrictions.

Show your work to anyone who might be interested in it. For instance, I include an image of my artwork on my business cards. You can also create postcards and brochures showcasing your talent. Give your art as much display time as you can in any form. Being timid about promoting your work will hurt you financially; don't pretend it won't. Here are a few things you can try:

- Approach local business owners and office spaces with lots of empty wall space and large volumes of visitors/collectors, such as; banks, coffee shops, bookstores, bars, restaurants, public library, office buildings, hospitals, community colleges, hotels etc. and ask if they would display a few pieces of your art. Many of them may already have rotating shows that you can apply for.

- Become a guest on a program sponsored by your local cable TV station. Create a discussion on a topic related to art where you can also showcase your artwork. At the end of the show they will usually allow you to give information on how to reach you. Another bonus is they will also give you a digital copy of your show that you can use for promotion, but you may need to ask for one if it is not offered.

- Participate in the "Art walks" if they are available in your town/city. Art walks give you and your artwork exposure in your community plus attendees enjoy buying art from local artists.

- Set up a booth at your local farmers and/or flea markets. Also check with the churches, schools, and fire departments for art fairs.

- Donate your art to non-profit organizations in your community for their fund raising events. Many non-profits hold art auctions to raise funds. Offering a work of art not only gives you exposure, but if you make a sale, you also know that you helped a worthy cause.

- Schmooze with the local press by sending emails and/or press releases to the editorial department of the local newspapers, newsletters, and radio stations. They can help you get the word out about your exhibits and projects, and it's free. In fact, it's not impossible to get a full page write up about your art if you are doing something unique and different, which is what happened to me a few years ago when I moved into a new town. I'm very open about letting people I meet know that I am an artist and the type of work I do. One person became so interested in my story they contacted a friend at the local newspaper which resulted in my art work being featured in a full page, color spread of the "Entertainment" section. Not only that, they heavily advertised the feature weeks before it came out. I became an instant celebrity and immediately established myself as a local artist.

- Register yourself and your artwork on the local, regional, and/or state Arts Registry. Every state has an Art Council which keeps a registry of artists in the state. Registration is free and can be usually done online. The Arts Registry is one of the places businesses, schools, and organizations refer to when looking for artists to participate in their events. For example, being on the state Arts Registry enabled me to receive an invitation for a solo exhibit in the state Governor's meeting room for a month. Individuals also use the registry for commissioned projects. One of the many benefits of being listed on the registry is you end up on their mailing list and are kept informed about art opportunities, events, and grants.

Go to http://www.nea.gov/partner/state/SAA_RAO_list.html for a list State, Regional, and jurisdictional Art agencies/councils.

Once you have increased your exposure and visibility in the community, start charging for your work. You want to establish the appearance of yourself as a working artist, first. The more exposure you get, the more people will associate you with your art. They can't buy from you if they don't know you exist. But, don't go to the extreme of never trying to sell your work. Remember every sell you

make helps you continue to finance what
you love to do.

Key #6
Commit to Excellence

What the art world does not need is another mediocre artist. In other words, don't settle for less when it comes to developing your skills. Take the time to be the best you can be. This means being willing to commit to putting in the hours and years of practice to become accomplished in your art. You will not be able to command a higher income/price for you art if you do not commit to excellence.

Art is a highly competitive field, but the good news for you is most people are not really serious about being successful. They consider art to be more of a hobby, not something they can seriously make a living from. After a year or less of half-heartedly trying, they will simply give up. They would much rather watch TV than to spend an extra hour mastering their art.

Consider landscape painting, for instance. There are millions of wannabe landscapes artists, but only a hand full of them are committed to becoming masters at it. They may buy all of the art supplies and practice now and then, but they lack the dedication to commit the years it will take to be successful. A popular landscape artist once said "You have to paint 300 bad paintings before you end up with a good one." Not many will want to continue after 10 or 12 bad paintings, let alone 300. These artists are not your competition so if you can seriously commit to your art for 3+ years, you will surpass the majority of them with your advanced skills that will easily get noticed above the rest.

All it takes is persistence and you can easily advance past 99% of the artists in your field. You begin to attract the opportunities and develop establishments that make it easier to generate income, the longer you work at and expose your art. For example, you will build your portfolio so you'll have more artwork to leverage; you'll increase your network of peers that help bring you more opportunities and who may even become your collectors.

So the question is, do you love art enough to commit to and invest 6,000 hours (about 3 years) full time to develop the skills needed to build a financially sustainable career as an artist? If you are not willing to make this type of commitment then you will join 99% of artists in any given field making little to no money from their art. Only the top 1% are financially successful because they are the ones willing to put in those 6,000 hours to become top in their field.

This may sound like a very difficult challenge to you now, but it is actually an easier commitment to make if you are passionate about your art. It only appears more difficult in the beginning. Remember, the actions you take today towards your creative goals are shaping your future for success.

Key #7
Keep Your Collectors Happy

It's nearly impossible to sustain yourself as an artist without creating a product that people want to buy consistently. So, if your art is not selling then you are not producing what your collectors want. You need to understand what they will buy and why.

Selling is a vital part of the creative process and begins with understanding who your audience is. You should ask yourself before starting a new project, "who will appreciate and buy my art?"

Try to meet your collectors or potential collectors face to face as often as possible and talk to them about what they want and what they like about your art work.

I enjoy taking the opportunity to talk to my potential collectors at the openings of my exhibits. I spend time getting to know their interest in art and what appeals to them about my work. I also find that when I tell them a story about the paintings, such as what inspired me and the process I used, it's easier to make a sell. Collectors enjoy making that connection with the artist whose work they invest in. And I enjoy learning something about the people who purchase my art. Taking the time to develop a strong relationship with your collectors will often ensure consistent sales from them.

It is important to create art that sells first, and not only creating art "for the Soul" or for the sheer joy of creating. Once you've built up your sales and collector base you will find there are buyers for just about anything you create.

Key #8
Support Your Fellow Artists

How often do you purchase art that you appreciate?

If you want to succeed as an artist you must support the belief that you deserve to be financially supported. You can reinforce that belief getting into the habit of financially supporting other artists whose work you appreciate and like.

It is also important not to pirate the work of artists if you wish others to respect and pay for your art work. Respect their right to ask for payment. I like to consider it my "expression of gratitude".

When I go to an artist exhibit or craft show, I try to find and purchase at least one work of art. If I see something I like but can't purchase it right then I get their business card or web address and purchase it later. There is a Universal truth that you have to be willing to give the very thing that you are wanting for yourself. It's amazing how uplifting I feel knowing I have helped support the creative endeavors of a follow artist.

Key #9
Accept Criticism Graciously

Nothing will slow down or bring your art career to a halt faster than your inability to accept criticism. I had a professor tell his art students "If you don't like criticism, than don't become an artist." In any one of the creative fields you are sure to find plenty of critics. You've heard the saying, "Those who can't do, teach". Well those who can't do also like to criticize the efforts of those who can. Of course, some critics will provide you with good advice for improvement and constructive feedback, even your friends and family. But, be aware you may often find their comments tinged with resentment and envy. Especially if you are really good at what you do and are recognized for it.

By trying to please critics, you give them the power to create within you; self-doubt, thoughts of failure, and beliefs of not feeling you are good enough. Nurturing self-doubt and internal negative thoughts are proven ways to stop your art career in its tracks. The secret to staying positive and prolific in your art is to give your full attention to your art, and less attention to the critics.

Ultimately, your critics can be safely ignored because they don't really provide value to what you do. But, like it or not, a critic can in some instances unintentionally elevate your status as an artist. For instance, when the criticism is primarily negative, it can help draw more attention to your art work, which benefits you with extra publicity. It will often get others talking and curious about your work. **The important thing for you to do is stay committed to your creative expression without defending your position. I find a little humor goes a long way. This will help keep the focus of attention on you. Otherwise, if you try to defend yourself, you release your power in the situation back to the critic.**

Look for opportunities to surround yourself with people who appreciate your art. I often find some of my best feedback comes from other artists, because they have a better understanding of the steps and challenges of going through the creative process. I still do not allow their feedback to override my own opinion, though. I only accept and keep what is useful for moving me forward in a positive way.

In the long run, honest constructive self-criticism is what you need to learn to give to your Self. Examine your art with a critical eye and pay close attention to your feelings about it. Frequently ask yourself, do you like the art you are creating? Do you enjoy doing it? If the answer is no, strive to understand why not. What improvements can you make to produce your best art ever? Examine your work with the intention of improving it instead of listening to the internal voice of self-doubt.

Key #10
Balance Your Relationship with Fans & Collectors

Unlike your critics, your fans and collectors are supporting your work and making it possible for you to keep doing what you love. Therefore, doesn't it make sense to assist them in supporting you?

First, it is important to understand the difference between fans and collectors. Your fans are those people who appreciate your art. They could easily be your family and friends. Your collectors are the ones who are financially supporting you as an artist. For example, you may have a large fan base of people on your Facebook page who follow and appreciate the art you create. But, they are not regular collectors. Although having a lot of fans may show your popularity and make you "famous", they are not going to sustain you financially unless you can convert them into collectors.

Maintaining loyal fans is still a wise decision and very easy to do through social media. Twitter is my favorite because it is not too time consuming (but additive) so I can quickly connect and respond to my fan base more frequently. Some artists feel it is smarter to put their collectors first if financial stability is the primary goal. I feel finding a balance between the two is a better way to go. But, either way will work depending on what your long term goals are. And finding what works best for you may take some time.

Your fans (non-collector) may not like it if you pay more attention to your collectors. They might feel unappreciated and abandon you as a result. Sure, you may possibly lose the chance to make them a collector in the future and/or lose new collectors they bring to you. But, there's really no guarantee these would have happened anyway. On the other hand, anyone with good business sense knows and understands the benefits of working hard to keep supportive collectors.

While it is important to appreciate your fans and collectors, it is important not to overdo it. As your art work becomes more popular the demands on your time and attention may feel overwhelming. You could end up resenting all the attention if you allow things to get out of control. With so many people wanting to connect with you it is important that you protect your sacred creative space and seek moments of solitude. Don't allow your fans, collectors, or anyone else to intrude upon your connection to the creator spirit within you. Trust that your fans and collectors will still accept you for not being as available to them. Communicate this need to them and help them understand it is necessary in order for you to create. For instance, the important people in my world know and understand when I withdraw for a while I am creating art and they are more than happy to honor and respect my space and "quiet time". Because they know when I emerge again, they have my attention and they get to enjoy my new works of art.

Conclusion

In conclusion, making a financially sustainable living as an artist is an achievable goal for those who are committed to the mastery of their art regardless of how long it takes. It doesn't require luck or sacrificing your artistic expression. But, it does require making some intelligent choices and having a strong unwavering commitment.

So you owe it to yourself to "just do it". Start right now, today, and begin putting these 10 essential keys into action towards your success as an artist.

Resources

Online Art Communities
http://www.artistdaily.com/
http://www.wetcanvas.com

Online Art Journals, Reviews, & Magazines
http://www.artdaily.com/
http://www.artforum.com/
http://www.artnews.com/
http://www.fineartconnoisseur.com/
http://www.canadianart.ca/
http://www.artinamericamagazine.com/
http://www.aiamagazine.com/
http://www.artandantiquesmag.com/
http://www.artforum.com/

Daily Artists
http://dailypaintworks.com/

About the Author

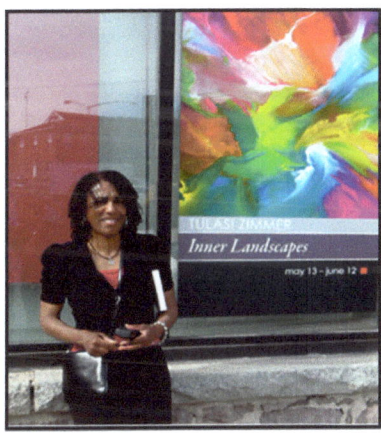

Tulasi (tul-see) Zimmer is a mid-career professional artist and educator. She grew up in Columbus, Ohio and earned a Bachelor of Fine Arts degree (BFA) from The Ohio State University and a Master of Fine Arts degree (MFA) from Miami University of Ohio in painting, drawing, and art history. Tulasi's professional art career includes experience as an illustrator; graphic designer; web developer; multimedia producer and publisher; computer animator; stained glass artist; fiber artist; and arts education administrator. She has created art and design for major corporations, publishers, State government, advertising agencies, institutions of higher education, and the private sector. Tulasi is an award winning oil painter with several national and regional awards and her art work belongs to public and private collections around the world.

Visit http://tulasizimmer.com